Silencing Voices

Book Bans, Cancel Culture, and Other Forms of Censorship

Robert Lerose

San Diego, CA

Printed in the United States

For more information, contact:
ReferencePoint Press, Inc.
PO Box 27779
San Diego, CA 92198
www.ReferencePointPress.com

LIBRARY OF CONGRESS CATALOGING-IN-PUBLICATION DATA

Author: Robert Lerose
Title: Silencing Voices: Book Bans, Cancel Culture, and Other Forms of Censorship
Description: San Diego, CA : ReferencePoint Press, 2026.
Includes bibliographical references and index
Identifiers: LCCN 2025003676 (print) | ISBN
9781678211981 library binding | ISBN 9781678211998 ebook

For compete cataloging-in-publication data please go to www.loc.gov.

The Fight Over the First Amendment

On March 25, 2022, Governor Ron DeSantis of Florida held a news conference on the campus of Embry-Riddle Aeronautical University in Daytona Beach. DeSantis was there to sign House Bill 1467, sometimes referred to as the curriculum transparency bill. The new law made it mandatory for school districts to be more open about the instructional materials students were exposed to, the books available to students in the school library, and the selections on required student reading lists.

The law also gave parents more power over what their children were taught or could read. Any parent or county resident—even just one person—who objected to any book for any reason could get that title removed and subjected to a formal review. "In Florida, our parents have every right to be involved in their child's education. We are not going to let politicians deny parents the right to know what is being taught in our schools,"[1] DeSantis says.

> **"We are not going to let politicians deny parents the right to know what is being taught in our schools."[1]**
>
> —Ron DeSantis, Florida governor

The law generated intense reactions, with some parents grateful that they had a greater say in their children's education. "I stand here today representing thousands of mothers and fathers who have felt voiceless. I am thankful for a governor that has the courage to lead with integrity and to partner with parents as we strive to raise the standard of excellence in our education system,"[2] said Alicia Farrant, an Orange County parent.

Others saw the law as a dangerous step toward censorship. "Florida now joins places like Russia and China, modern-day examples of what happens when free thought and free speech are tightly restricted in all levels of society, including in school,"[3] says state senator Lauren Book, a parent and former teacher.

> **"Florida now joins places like Russia and China, modern-day examples of what happens when free thought and free speech are tightly restricted in all levels of society, including in school."[3]**
>
> —Lauren Book, Florida state senator

After the law went into effect, the American Library Association and the free speech group PEN America reported that book banning attempts jumped in Florida. In response, DeSantis modified the law in April 2024. Under the new provision, people without children in school could make only one challenge per month, but parents could still file an unlimited number.

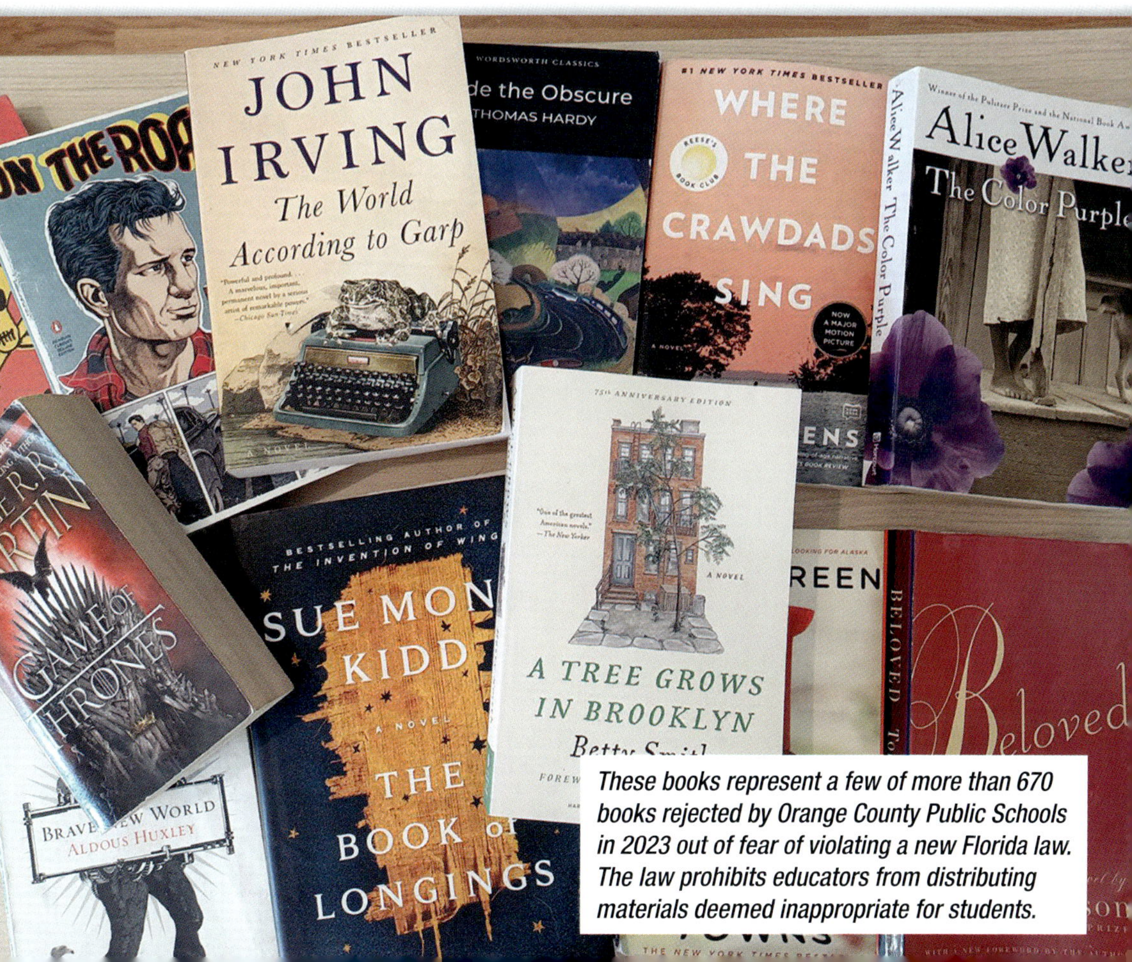

These books represent a few of more than 670 books rejected by Orange County Public Schools in 2023 out of fear of violating a new Florida law. The law prohibits educators from distributing materials deemed inappropriate for students.

Free Expression Under Fire

The conflict in Florida is just one example of a larger debate taking place in US society over free expression, a cornerstone of American civil liberties. Efforts to censor certain topics, words, and ideas have been growing in different settings.

Like school libraries, public libraries are also under intense pressure to remove books that some people view as objectionable, especially books aimed at younger audiences that discuss gender identity, drug use, mental illness, or sex. Librarians who have tried to defend the necessity of keeping these books available for all readers have often been harassed. "There were comments about library staff, calling us groomers and pedophiles and saying we needed to be fired, we need to be jailed, we needed to be locked up, that all the books needed to be burned,"[4] says Tonya Ryals, assistant director of the Jonesboro Public Library in Craighead County, Arkansas. In the face of these attacks, Ryals quit her job.

In the digital realm, regulating content on social media platforms has grown into a fierce dispute. Forums like X, formerly Twitter, are private companies and not subject to First Amendment compliance. Nevertheless, some say that these platforms should police posted content that contains misinformation or hate. The Foundation for Individual Rights and Expression takes a different view, saying "that the First Amendment protects the right of all private publishers, from printing press operators to Instagram, to selectively edit, curate, and publish content free from government intrusion."[5]

College campuses have been the scene of disagreements over the free expression of ideas as well. For example, divisions were made apparent after Hamas attacked Israel on October 7, 2023. Pro-Israeli and pro-Palestinian demonstrations erupted on many colleges and universities across the country. The heated rhetoric in these rallies drew greater attention to the debate over what constitutes legally protected speech versus hate-mongering. College leaders found themselves in a bind, torn between respecting students' First Amendment rights to voice their individual opinions and ensuring a safe and secure learning environment for all. Some college presidents and administrators either resigned or were fired over the positions they took.

There have also been many instances of speakers who have been invited to address university communities only to be disinvited and their speaking engagement canceled because certain student groups objected to the speaker's message or viewpoint. For example, in the spring of 2024, the University of Southern California prohibited graduating senior Asna Tabassum, a South Asian American Muslim, from delivering the valedictory address at commencement after pro-Israeli groups opposed some of her pro-Palestinian political positions. "I am not surprised by those who attempt to propagate hatred. I am surprised that my own university—my home for four years—has abandoned me,"[6] says Tabassum.

Free speech is a fundamental right that is a pillar of American democracy, but it is not unlimited. Debates concerning free speech typically focus on where those limits lie. While these discussions address politics and philosophy, their outcomes have real-world consequences. Censorship, book banning, and cancel culture influence how people access information and express themselves, ultimately reflecting the values Americans uphold and the causes they are willing to defend.

An Essential Right

Of all the rights guaranteed to Americans, the right to free speech is among the most cherished. Free expression is so important that the Founding Fathers enshrined it in the First Amendment to the US Constitution. The amendment gives people protection under the law to express even unpopular or controversial views without fear. But free speech is not an absolute, unlimited right. Even the original framers of American rights debated the scope of free speech and expression.

The Road to Free Speech

The First Amendment was the product of revision and compromise. As with the Declaration of Independence and the US Constitution itself, the founders argued over the amendment's wording. In his original draft of the First Amendment submitted to the House of Representatives on June 8, 1789, James Madison wrote, "The people shall not be deprived or abridged of their right to speak, to write, or to publish their sentiments; and the freedom of the press, as one of the great bulwarks of liberty, shall be inviolable."[7]

A House committee rewrote Madison's draft to include the right to peacefully assemble and to redress grievances against the government. The Senate would further expand these protections to cover freedom of religion, which finally led to the adoption of the amendment's current language.

For Thomas Jefferson, ensuring free speech was essential for a democratic government to function. According to him, free speech enabled people to criticize those in power without fear of retaliation and therefore keep authorities accountable.

Benjamin Franklin concurred when he said, "Without freedom of thought, there can be no such thing as wisdom; and no such thing as public liberty, without freedom of speech."[8] To that end, the founders created broad protections for most—but not all—forms of expression.

> **"Without freedom of thought, there can be no such thing as wisdom; and no such thing as public liberty, without freedom of speech."[8]**
>
> —Benjamin Franklin

Like the debate over the amendment's wording, these protections were not perfectly formed at once but evolved over time. Originally, the First Amendment only barred the federal government from taking any actions that could undermine these protections, but it was a different matter for the individual states. Each state had the authority to develop its own laws and enforce them through its own state courts. This changed in 1868 with the adoption of the Fourteenth Amendment to the US Constitution, which prohibited state actions that denied people "liberty" without "due process." Put another way, the amendment restricted the states from making any laws that infringed on any rights spelled out in the US Constitution—including the right to free expression.

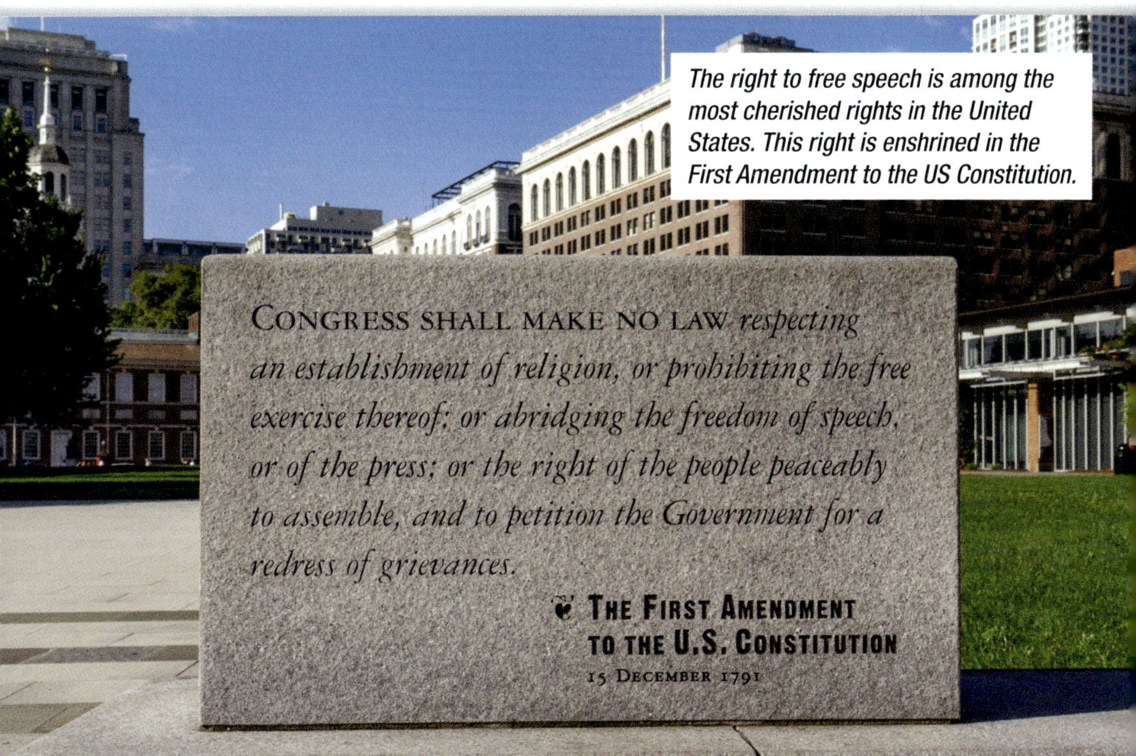

The right to free speech is among the most cherished rights in the United States. This right is enshrined in the First Amendment to the US Constitution.

In a series of rulings in the twentieth century, the US Supreme Court held that the First Amendment was binding on all levels of government—local, state, and federal. These legislative and judicial acts were a check on the power of government, a concern of the founders. As a result, First Amendment protections are upheld across a wide range of institutions: all branches of government, legislatures, courts, public employers, public universities, and public school systems. But these protections do not apply to the private sector, and therefore, there is no guarantee of free speech in privately held companies or private universities. That is why, for example, internet service providers, which are nongovernment entities, can refuse to host certain websites or why employees at a local for-profit business do not enjoy free speech protections at their workplace.

Speech That Causes Harm

Under the First Amendment, people possess enormous freedom to have their ideas heard and circulated. Speech having to do with religion, science, art, or morality—even language that could be considered racist—is protected. Writers of opinion pieces, such as newspaper columnists who speak their mind on an issue or public figure, enjoy great freedom even if their opinions are arguably harsh, excessively negative, or critical.

Still, the First Amendment does not protect every form of expression in every situation. Some restrictions are necessary for the welfare of all and for society to function. To that end, the government and courts have established certain norms that respect both freedom of expression and public safety and social order. In practice, the government cannot censor political speech, such as when people protest a war. On the other hand, the government does have the right to restrict when and where a speech is given, provided that the restriction has nothing to do with the content of the speech. During the 2024 Republican and Democratic conventions, for example, free speech zones were set up away from the convention sites—allowing protesters to express their views

The Free Speech Rights of Students

The Vietnam War was a controversial military action that divided America. Protests of the war took place frequently, many organized by young people of draft age and eligible to be sent overseas to fight. To show their support for an end to the war, a group of public school students in Des Moines, Iowa, agreed to wear black armbands to school during the December 1965 holiday season. School administrators quickly passed a policy prohibiting the wearing of armbands and suspending students who refused to comply. Sixteen-year-old Christopher Eckhardt, fifteen-year-old John Tinker, and his thirteen-year-old sister, Mary Beth Tinker, were sent home when they showed up at school wearing armbands. The students and their parents sued the school district, but two lower courts said that the school acted reasonably and was only trying to maintain order. The case made its way to the US Supreme Court in November 1968. On February 24, 1969, the court ruled 7–2 in favor of the students, finding that the armbands were a form of expression protected by the First Amendment. In his majority opinion, Associate Justice Abe Fortas wrote, "It can hardly be argued that either students or teachers shed their constitutional rights to freedom of speech or expression at the schoolhouse gate."

Quoted in *Tinker v. Des Moines Independent Community School District*, 393 U.S. 503 (1969).

but keeping them from disrupting the main events. Along these same lines, the government can restrict picketing in front of a person's house or a demonstration that interferes with the flow of traffic. Such forms of expression could cause harm or infringe on other fundamental rights and are therefore regulated by law.

Speech that might be considered inflammatory or reckless or meant to incite violence has perplexed legal scholars, sparking ongoing debate over whether it deserves protection under the law. One of the earliest cases to explore this question was *Schenck v. United States*, argued in 1919 before the US Supreme Court. During World War I, Charles Schenck and Elizabeth Baer were arrested for distributing literature that opposed the draft and military service. When they were convicted under the Espionage Act of 1917, they argued that their First Amendment right to free speech had been violated. In a unanimous ruling, the justices denied their claim. Writing the opinion for the court, Justice Oliver Wendell Holmes Jr. famously said, "The most stringent protection of free speech would not protect a man in falsely shouting fire in a theatre and causing a panic." In the court's

"The most stringent protection of free speech would not protect a man in falsely shouting fire in a theatre and causing a panic."[9]

—Oliver Wendell Holmes Jr., US Supreme Court justice

view, the necessities of wartime mobilization produced an environment in which anti-draft rhetoric would impede the nation from preparing for global conflict. Holmes added, "The question in every case is whether the words used are used in such circumstances and are of such a nature as to create a clear and present danger that they will bring about the substantive evils that Congress has a right to prevent."[9] By this ruling, the First Amendment would not protect an individual who knowingly disrupted the government from pursuing an arguably greater good.

Danger to the Public

Building on Holmes's "clear and present danger" measure, other forms of speech have been restricted. For instance, speech can be prohibited if it contains the threat of an imminent unlawful action, because it represents a clear and present danger. Those who make such threats can be prosecuted and held accountable. However, the law makes an exception: if the speaker who advocates an unlawful action does not specify a date for said action—but only vaguely refers to some future time—then the speech is permissible.

In 1969 this exception was tested when the US Supreme Court took up another free speech case, *Brandenburg v. Ohio*. Clarence Brandenburg was a Ku Klux Klan leader in Ohio who was convicted for giving a speech that called for the forced expulsion of Blacks and Jews from America. The Supreme Court disagreed, saying that Brandenburg's First Amendment rights had been violated because it was not clear that his speech would lead to unlawful actions. In a unanimous decision, the court said, in part, "The constitutional guarantees of free speech and free press do not permit a State to forbid or proscribe advocacy of the use of force or of law violation except where such advocacy is directed to inciting or producing imminent lawless action and is likely to incite or produce such action."[10] In Brandenburg's case it was not obvious that his words would persuade people to embrace violence as a means to reform and that vague advocacy for the use of force—even to overthrow the government—is not a punishable offense.

Free Speech During Wartime

The legal decisions handed down by the US Supreme Court use imminent danger as a standard for determining whether provocative speech should be allowed or restricted. The standard is helpful, but reasonable parties can still have an honest disagreement about whether the release of certain speech would result in an imminent risk to the public or the nation. This was the debate that swirled around the case of the so-called Pentagon Papers. The *Report of the Office of the Secretary of Defense Vietnam Task Force* was a forty-seven-volume history, spanning the period from World War II to 1968, of America's involvement in Vietnam and the war that followed. Daniel Ellsberg, a researcher who worked on compiling the history, became disenchanted with how US presidential administrations were withholding the full story from the American public about the war. Ellsberg took classified information from the report and shared it with the *New York Times*.

A 1970 photograph shows American troops running toward a helicopter during the Vietnam War. The government tried to block the New York Times *from publishing the Pentagon Papers, a lengthy history of America's involvement in Vietnam.*

When the *New York Times* began publishing what popularly became known as the Pentagon Papers on June 13, 1971, the US Department of Justice got a court order to halt publication. John Mitchell, the US attorney general at the time, warned the *New York Times* that distributing the classified material would lead to "irreparable injury to the defense interests of the United States."[11] The newspaper disagreed, believing that the public had a right to know. On June 30, in a 6–3 decision, the US Supreme Court held in favor of the *New York Times*. In his opinion supporting the ruling, Justice Hugo Black wrote, "In the First Amendment, the Founding Fathers gave the free press the protection it must have to fulfill its essential role in our democracy."[12] To Black, that role was to provide a safeguard against governmental tyranny and deception.

> **"In the First Amendment, the Founding Fathers gave the free press the protection it must have to fulfill its essential role in our democracy."[12]**
>
> —Hugo Black, US Supreme Court justice

Freedom of the Press

Putting free speech in the First Amendment demonstrated the founders' belief in its importance. The controversy surrounding the Pentagon Papers proved that equally important is freedom of the press. The founders believed that this freedom would enable news services to report and distribute opinion, commentary, and analysis on any topic or about any individual without fear of censorship. As Black affirmed, it allows the press to criticize things in the public interest and to hold parties accountable, whether a political leader who might be stealing or a business involved in illegal polluting. Even though the press has this enormous power, it is still bound to use it responsibly. The press cannot intentionally publish something that it knows to be false. Falsehoods that appear in print and that defame any party are known as libel. When people or institutions think that they have been defamed, they can sue the publication on those grounds.

Historically, winning a defamation suit against the press is difficult. News outlets know the limitations of their power and of what they can print. Unless there is an obvious disregard for the truth, the press is free to publish stories in the public's interest. Freedom of the press extends to all legitimate news organizations—not only to institutions like the *New York Times*, Fox News, and National Public Radio, but also to school newspapers. All these face libel suits when victims feel their rights have been abused, but proving the abuse requires pinpointing the falsehoods. For example, in July 2023 Tamara Kay, a professor at the University of Notre Dame, filed a lawsuit against the *Irish Rover*, an independent student newspaper. The *Rover* had published articles reporting on Kay's pro-abortion advocacy and her offers to help students who needed an abortion. Kay sued the *Rover* over what she said were defamatory and false statements in the articles that prompted some readers to harass her and even damage her residence. After reviewing the evidence, the St. Joseph County Superior Court found that the articles were fact based and complied with the law. The case against the *Rover* and the reporters was dismissed.

Sarah Palin's Libel Lawsuit

On January 8, 2011, Jared Lee Loughner fired into a crowd at a Tucson supermarket. He seriously wounded US representative Gabrielle Giffords and killed six bystanders. In a June 2017 editorial following another gun attack on politicians, James Bennet of the *New York Times* wrote that before the Tucson shooting, the political action committee for former Republican vice presidential nominee Sarah Palin put out a map with gun-sight crosshairs over vulnerable Democratic politicians. The editorial claimed that Palin's rhetoric may have led to Loughner's rampage. Two days later, the *New York Times* corrected mistakes in the editorial and said that "no connection" between Loughner and Palin's map had been confirmed—but Palin believed she had been defamed. Palin sued the newspaper for libel but lost. She appealed the ruling and in August 2024 was granted a new trial. Palin's lawyer hoped to show that Bennet acted recklessly or knew that what he was writing was false. The lawyer described the new trial as "a significant step forward in the process of holding publishers accountable for content that misleads readers and the public in general." In April 2025 a federal jury rejected Palin's claim that the editorial defamed her.

Quoted in David Enrich, "Sarah Palin Is Granted New Libel Trial Against the *New York Times*," *New York Times*, September 26, 2024. www.nytimes.com.

Penalties for Libel and Slander

Getting the facts straight before criticizing someone in print is essential. Otherwise, there could be serious consequences. Michael Mann, a climate scientist at Pennsylvania State University, found this out when he created a graph that showed how burning fossil fuels had historically resulted in rising global temperatures. Rand Simberg, a policy analyst, and Mark Steyn, an author, published online posts that called Mann's work fraudulent and accused him of rigging the data to arrive at his findings, but they did not have convincing evidence to back up their claims. Mann sued Simberg and Steyn for libel and won his case in February 2024, when he was awarded over $1 million in damages. "I hope this verdict sends a message that falsely attacking climate scientists is not protected speech,"[13] Mann says.

Libel, or written speech that contains falsehoods, is just one form of defamation. Slander, or spoken speech that defames a

Infowars creator and host Alex Jones (pictured in 2010) repeatedly told his listeners that the deadly 2012 mass shooting at Sandy Hook Elementary School was staged. Courts in at least two states have ruled that Jones defamed the families by making repeated false claims about the shooting.

person, can also be cause for legal action. A recent example that garnered a lot of attention involved Alex Jones and families of the Sandy Hook school shooting victims. On his radio show and podcast, Jones repeatedly told his listeners that the massacre at Sandy Hook was staged and that the young victims of the shooting were part of an elaborate hoax. As a result of his comments, many of the parents of the murdered children reported being threatened, harassed, and endangered by Jones's followers who believed his lies. "I fear for my life, I fear for my safety,"[14] said Neil Heslin, father of a six-year-old killed at Sandy Hook. The families sued Jones for defamation, and in 2021 a judge ruled in their favor. Jones was eventually ordered to pay over $1 billion in damages, a judgment he is contesting.

The Founding Fathers recognized free speech as a pillar of American democracy. Since its ratification in December 1791 to the present day, the limitations, meaning, and intent of the First Amendment have been debated in the courts and in public forums. Reasonable parties may disagree over legal decisions interpreting it, but the freedom to express oneself without fear remains an enduring American value.

The Movement to Ban Books

Suzette Baker loved being the head librarian at Kingsland Public Library in Llano County, Texas, about 65 miles (105 km) from Austin. She enjoyed putting up book displays tied to holidays or themes and helping library patrons find the perfect book for their interests. In November 2021 Baker got a disturbing order from library administrators. Bonnie Wallace, a member of the Llano County library advisory board, had demanded the removal of all books from the library that "depict any type of sexual activity or questionable nudity," calling them "pornographic filth."[15]

Among the books singled out for removal were *Being Jazz: My Life as a (Transgender) Teen*; *It's Perfectly Normal: Changing Bodies, Growing Up, Sex and Sexual Health*; *Freakboy*; and *Larry the Farting Leprechaun*. Baker refused on the grounds that removing the books violated the First Amendment. "This was never about the books. This was never about protecting people. The books that they gave me to get rid of were books on racism. They were books on transgender and sexual orientation and questioning for teens,"[16] Baker says.

She was subsequently fired in March 2022 for insubordination. Despite the personal and emotional toll on her life, taking a stand against this type of censorship was a no-brainer for Baker. "I know what I did was right,"[17] she says. In April 2022 a federal lawsuit was filed by seven county residents who objected to the book ban. The following March an appeals court judge ordered eight of the seventeen banned books returned to the shelves, with nine books remaining off the shelves while the county contested the ruling. A federal court of appeals began hearing oral arguments for the case in September 2024.

Book Bans on the Rise

Efforts to ban or restrict access to books are happening across the country in growing numbers. The American Library Association (ALA) has seen an uptick in book censorship in the past few years. In 2023 there was a 65 percent jump in the number of titles in danger of being removed from schools and libraries compared to 2022. This put 4,240 unique book titles at risk—a record number since the association began collecting this data. "Each demand to ban a book is a demand to deny each person's constitutionally protected right to choose and read books that raise important issues and lift up the voices of those who

Book Bans Have Grown

Efforts to ban books have risen dramatically over a nineteen-year period. According to the American Library Association's Office of Intellectual Freedom, relatively few books were challenged in the early 2000s. That changed starting in 2021. Between 2022 and 2023 alone, the number of challenges increased 65 percent.

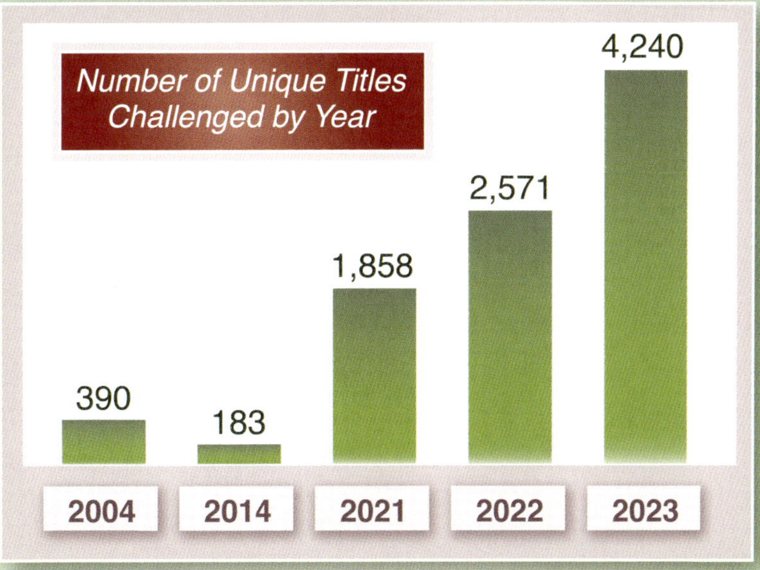

Source: "Censorship by the Numbers," American Library Association: Banned and Challenged Books. www.ala.org/bbooks/censorship-numbers.

"Each demand to ban a book is a demand to deny each person's constitutionally protected right to choose and read books that raise important issues and lift up the voices of those who are often silenced."[18]

—Deborah Caldwell-Stone, director of the American Library Association's Office for Intellectual Freedom

are often silenced,"[18] says Deborah Caldwell-Stone, director of ALA's Office for Intellectual Freedom.

Denying access to a book can take a few forms. Most of the time when a book is restricted or removed, it usually refers to a title found at a public or school library or on the reading list of a school curriculum. The ALA draws a distinction between a challenge and a banning. According to the ALA, "A challenge is an attempt to remove or restrict materials, based upon the objections of a person or group. A banning is the removal of those materials. Challenges do not simply involve a person expressing a point of view; rather, they are an attempt to remove material from the curriculum or library, thereby restricting the access of others."[19]

Typically, anyone can challenge a book at a public library by submitting a formal complaint. The library staff reviews the complaint and then determines how the matter should be handled. Sometimes the book might be removed from the shelf and placed in a restricted area. Other times, the objection to the book could be turned down and the book returned to open circulation. To object to a book in a public school library, the requirements may vary. Some districts allow only parents who have children in the school system the option of filing an unlimited number of complaints. Citizens without children in attendance may be restricted in how many book complaints they can make.

Common Content Targeted

An individual or a group that challenges a book can do so for almost any reason. Still, there do seem to be certain objections that come up often in these complaints. PEN America, an organization founded in 1922 that fights to protect free expression and the rights of creators, looked at the books that were banned in the 2022–2023 academic year. According to its findings, these titles were removed primarily because the content contained themes of violence or abuse; dealt with issues of mental health, bullying, suicide, or substance abuse; described the sexual experiences of characters; explored issues of race and racism; dealt with LGBTQ characters or themes; or described episodes of grief or death. "Book bans are targeting narratives about race and sexual identities and sexual content writ large, and they show no sign of stopping. The bans we're seeing are broad, harsh and pernicious—and they're undermining the education of millions of students across the country,"[20] says Sabrina Baêta, Freedom to Read program manager at PEN America.

> **"The bans we're seeing are broad, harsh and pernicious—and they're undermining the education of millions of students across the country."[20]**
>
> —Sabrina Baêta, Freedom to Read program manager at PEN America

Schools and libraries are dealing with an unprecedented surge in censorship of reading materials. From July 1, 2021, to December 31, 2023, PEN America recorded book banning activities in forty-two of the fifty states. In some of these instances, state governments have made it significantly easier for the complaint process to result in the removal of a title. A prime example is a new law in Utah that went into effect in July 2024. Under the new law, a book

Censorship of books and other reading material has been growing in schools and libraries in many parts of the nation. These efforts are limiting students' freedom to read about a wide array of topics.

"This is a big win because now I can send my kid, you can send your child to school and know that these 13 titles which went through a very rigorous process are no longer available to kids in that school."[22]

—Corinne Johnson, president of Utah Parents United

can be banned in schools statewide if only three school district boards object to the book because in their view it contains material that lacks "literary, artistic, political or scientific value for minors."[21]

Within a month of the law's passage, thirteen books were removed from school library shelves, including works by popular authors such as Judy Blume, Ellen Hopkins, and Sarah J. Maas. The law required that the books be disposed of permanently. Also, the law stipulates that only a member of the Utah State Board of Education could request a hearing to consider returning a banned book. Supporters of the book ban celebrated the new law. "This is a big win because now I can send my kid, you can send your child to school and know that these 13 titles which went through a very rigorous process are no longer available to kids in that school,"[22]

Writer Judy Blume appears at the 2023 movie premiere of her popular young adult book, Are You There God? It's Me, Margaret. *Under a 2024 Utah law, books by Blume and other popular authors were removed from school libraries.*

The Librarian and the Death Threat

Amanda Jones was proud to be a middle school librarian in her hometown of Watson, Louisiana. She was upset when she heard that the local public library was considering banning LGBTQ books, and she understood the hurtful impact it would have on LGBTQ students. On July 19, 2022, she addressed the library board at a public meeting and "reminded them, regardless of their own beliefs on the topic of book content and location, to think about this: no one on the right side of history has ever been on the side of censorship and hiding books." About three weeks later, she got an email that used abusive language and warned, "You have a LARGE target on your back." Jones was petrified. She could not understand how a stranger would threaten her life because she stood up for other people's right to read, but felt she had an obligation to continue to speak out. "I figure if people are going to label me an activist, I might as well act like one and show them what I'm made of—grit and perseverance," she says. "Hell hath no fury like a librarian scorned."

Quoted in Amanda Jones, "I Spoke Out Against Library Book Bans. Then the Death Threats Started," Oprah Daily, August 27, 2024. www.oprahdaily.com.

says Corinne Johnson, president of Utah Parents United, an advocacy group for parental rights.

But others saw the law as an infringement on young people's freedoms. "Allowing just a handful of districts to make decisions for the whole state is antidemocratic, and we are concerned that implementation of the law will result in less diverse library shelves for all Utahns,"[23] says Kasey Meehan of PEN America.

Parental Rights Groups and Censorship

Many of the efforts to ban books are being spearheaded by so-called parental rights groups, such as Utah Parents United. These groups are dedicated to giving parents more information about what their children are being taught, the reading material assigned in the curriculum, and the books available in public school libraries and classrooms. With this information, they believe, parents can have a greater voice in their children's education and the content they are exposed to.

Some of these groups are national in scope. Founded in January 2021, Moms for Liberty is a nonprofit organization whose stated mission is "fighting for the survival of America by unifying, educating and empowering parents to defend their parental rights at all levels of government."[24] The group reportedly has chapters in almost every state, making it one of the largest parental rights organizations and capable of influencing book censorship issues around the country. The *Guardian* reported that "according to a 2023 PEN America report, 81% of school districts that banned books between July 2002 and June 2023 were within or adjoined a county with a local chapter of a group such as Moms for Liberty."[25]

Critics of Moms for Liberty, such as the Foundation for Individual Rights and Expression (FIRE), believe these parental rights organizations are engaged in censorship of viewpoints that do not conform to their own. They point to the group's objection to reading material dealing with LGBTQ and racial justice issues in school curricula. "Moms for Liberty is simply continuing the time-honored tradition of perpetuating the very kind of censorship that the First Amendment stands to prevent,"[26] FIRE argues. There is widespread agreement that parents have a right to control what their children read, but critics argue that when parents or groups claiming to represent their interests demand the removal of reading material from library shelves, they effectively deprive other families of the right to decide what is appropriate for their own children.

Students Defy the Censors

Efforts to ban books or even restrict access to them are on the rise, but they are not going unchallenged. Organizations like the ALA and PEN America, which have long histories of resisting book bans, are leaders in the fight. However, student groups opposed to censorship are standing up as well and fighting for the freedom to read what they want.

In the fall of 2020, some parents in the Central York School District in Pennsylvania began to object to classroom material that had to do with diversity, equity, and inclusion; the civil rights movement; and LGBTQ issues. In response, the school board put together a list of about three hundred items—books such as *I Am Rosa Parks* and *Pride: The Story of Harvey Milk & the Rainbow Flag*—that teachers were prohibited from using in their classrooms. "What we are attempting to do is balance legitimate academic freedom with what could be literature/materials that are too activist in nature, and may lean more toward indoctrination rather than age-appropriate academic content,"[27] said Jane Johnson, president of the Central York school board at the time.

As an Indian American student, Edha Gupta could never remember being assigned a book at Central York High School that portrayed her ethnic experiences. She felt left out and isolated from fellow students. When Gupta heard about the widespread book ban ordered by the local school board, she could not sit idle. Teaming up with a teacher/student activist group on campus, Gupta convinced fellow students to show up at school wearing black T-shirts as one way to show their anger with the school's censorship decision. Students would also protest for fifteen minutes every morning before classes started. After two weeks, the Central York school board suspended the ban and reinstated the materials for classroom use. The decision and the victory were bittersweet for Gupta. "It is just disheartening to know how much

Ninety-Seven Books Pulled

As she settled into her Advanced Placement literature class in Beaufort High School in South Carolina in 2022, Millie Bennett got some disturbing news. Her school district was removing ninety-seven books from school libraries after some parents complained that they contained "sexually explicit or inappropriate" subject matter. It was particularly upsetting to Bennett because she was a queer teen and some of the titles covered LGBTQ issues. Bennett was president of the Diversity Awareness Youth Literacy Organization chapter at her school, a student-run group committed to building tolerance and understanding among people through books. She and fellow members began speaking out against the book removal at school board meetings and pressed their case with lawmakers at the South Carolina statehouse. Eventually, all but five of the books were returned to the shelves. "I really wish this wasn't something that [fell] to the students. But as I see it, the students are the most impactful voice in this, and they are the ones being directly impacted. So they have the most important things to say," Bennett says.

Quoted in Eesha Pendharker, "What Happened When Students Led Fights to Reverse Book Bans," *Education Week*, July 18, 2023. www.edweek.org.

was required to put into that to make that happen, but at the same time, I'm so happy that we were able to make this tangible change,"[28] Gupta says.

Students are finding new ways to make their voices heard and protect their freedom to read. In New York in 2022, Orchard Park High School sophomores Luke Lippitt and Jillian Yarnes were alarmed to learn that some parents were demanding the removal of certain books from the district's libraries. In response, they founded Students Protecting Education, an organization that advocates for an education system built around diversity, equity, and inclusion. Lippitt and Yarnes, with fellow student and cofounder Claire Kent, spoke in front of about three hundred people—roughly split between those in favor of and those against the book removal—at a November 2022 school board meeting. "I'm standing here in front of you all in opposition of the outrageous efforts to suppress and censor ideas and to defend the right of my peers to decide for themselves what they are capable of reading,"[29] Lippitt said.

At the end of the meeting, David Lilleck, the Orchard Park School District superintendent, said that these books were valuable for all students because they reflect the experiences and sensibilities of different communities in life-affirming ways. Parents could keep their own children from reading material they disagreed with but not other parents' children. In July 2024 Lippitt was appointed to the Orchard Park Board of Education, pledging to fight for the organization's values of diversity and inclusiveness.

The ALA has reported an alarming rise in the number of book challenges and removals in just the past few years. And PEN America claims that 60 percent of bans are focused on young adult titles, meaning that the controversy over book censorship will most prominently affect young people. In response, some young people are voicing their opposition to these book bans and siding with long-established organizations to protect the First Amendment freedom of expression and the right to read what they want.

Censorship in the Classroom

Restricting, removing, or banning reading material from libraries and classrooms around the country has surged in the past few years. But censorship also affects what is being taught in schools, with heated arguments over what is "appropriate" or "inappropriate" content for classroom discussion. The stakes are high for all the parties involved, including government leaders, educators, parents, and students.

Controlling the Curriculum

Changes to educational curricula are nothing new to schools and school boards. Classroom curricula have been regularly revised or changed to meet new educational standards. In other instances, a curriculum may be updated to reflect new scholarship in a field or developments in the real world. For example, a science textbook used in classrooms in 2000 would probably have little or no information on artificial intelligence, but a current science curriculum would likely have an in-depth section on the topic because of its prevalence today.

However, while updates are expected, curricula are now regularly scrutinized for the type of information they contain and the viewpoints they share. Some people believe that schools teach topics that are inappropriate for young people or present a skewed version of history—at least, one that does not match their own views. For these reasons, history curricula have recently come under fire. Who controls the historical narrative—deciding which stories should be told and how—is the focus of the debate over classroom curricula.

The teaching of history has attracted a great deal of scrutiny in many school districts. Deciding which stories should be told and how to tell them is the focus of the debate over classroom curricula.

The most prominent discussions highlight sensitive issues and how they are presented in the classroom to students. According to the Brookings Institution, a nonpartisan research organization, by the spring of 2024, "20 states [had] enacted restrictions on how teachers can discuss so-called 'divisive concepts'—including race, gender, gender identity, and sexual orientation—in classrooms, affecting roughly 1.3 million teachers and 20 million students."[30] These restrictions have not met with unanimous approval. Although they have been challenged and revised in some states, Florida has gone in another direction.

Rewriting History

Since 1994 Florida's public schools had been required by law to teach African American history. But in 2023 a state task force found that many districts fell far short of the recommended education standards for teaching the history of Black Americans. These results were released following new legislation in 2022 that curbed how race could be discussed in classrooms. In reaction to widespread diversity, equity, and inclusion measures—what some critics referred to as a "woke" ideology—the legislature passed the Individual Freedom Act. On April 22, 2022, Governor Ron DeSantis signed the bill into law at a ceremony at Mater Academy Charter Middle/High School in Hialeah Gardens, saying, "We believe in education, not indoctrination."[31]

The Individual Freedom law prohibits any instruction that might make a student feel "guilt, anguish, or other forms of psychological distress because of actions, in which the person played no part, committed in the past by other members of the same race, color, national origin, or sex."[32]

The law forbids any instruction that might lead to the conclusion that "a person, by virtue of his or her race, color, national origin, or sex is inherently racist, sexist, or oppressive, whether consciously or unconsciously."[33] Real-world instances of alleged guilt-inducing instruction in Florida classrooms have been hard to come by. But in a hypothetical example, Florida state senator Manny Díaz Jr. said any teacher who taught that White students were somehow responsible for slavery because of the actions of their White ancestors would be in violation of the law. The Individual Freedom law is not a blanket prohibition on discussion of race. The Florida Senate points out that exceptions to these restrictions, under the law, are allowed when "training or instruction may include a discussion of such concepts if they are presented in an objective manner without endorsement."[34]

The law's provisions were put to the test a year later. In 2023 the Florida Board of Education issued new guidance for Black history instruction. The board now mandated that middle school teachers frame slavery in a more positive light by telling students that slaves picked up valuable skills during their forced servitude that would serve them well in their lives.

When these revised requirements were made public, they were criticized by the Florida Education Association, a statewide teachers' union. Other educators and scholars agreed that they presented students with an inaccurate, distorted view of an ugly

A young slave is auctioned off in South Carolina around 1780. In 2023 Florida education officials instructed the state's middle school teachers to frame slavery in a more positive light.

period in American history and that the new guidelines did not address the long history of oppression and intimidation against slaves in particular and Black people in general. According to Derrick Johnson, president of the National Association for the Advancement of Colored People, these requirements "are an attempt to bring our country back to a 19th century America where Black life was not valued, nor our rights protected. It is imperative that we understand that . . . slavery and Jim Crow . . . represent the darkest period in American history."[35] Some individuals are relieved that support for this type of revisionist history is not widespread. A 2022 Ipsos poll for ParentsTogether, a nonprofit organization focused on family issues, found that "most Americans (86%) and parents (87%) feel lessons about the history of racism prepare children to build a better future for everyone."[36]

Gender Controversy

Along with race, gender issues and their discussion in the classroom have also made news. Disagreements about how gender should be taught, or even if it should be taught, have flared up in school districts across the country. Some believe that the proper place to address questions of gender or gender identity is in the home, letting parents decide what to tell their children. Others think that children and young adults who have questions or who are struggling with their sexual identity should be able to find a safe space in the schoolhouse to explore their concerns.

Some states have taken legal action to regulate classroom discussions of gender identity and sex. In June 2024 Louisiana governor Jeff Landry signed House Bill 122 into law for public school students in grades K–12. Under this legislation, known as Let Kids Be Kids, the presentation of gender or sexuality topics must follow state-approved curriculum guidelines. For example, after the law went into effect, teachers were not allowed to talk about their own sexual identity, and after-school clubs were prohibited from covering sexual orientation or gender identity topics. Some are worried that the prohibition could threaten or even outlaw the existence of Gay-Straight Alliance organizations on campuses. But those in favor of the law maintain that its focus is to

Curriculum Partners

In July 2022 Idaho enacted a law requiring that at least half the members of any committee in charge of picking texts or classroom material be parents of school-age children or other community members. The other half would consist of state educators. In Twin Falls, the school district had usually included parents in the review and selection process, but this law made that arrangement mandatory. Some teachers objected, arguing that parents were not qualified to know the texts and other materials needed to teach a subject properly. Others worried that a community member might reject a text that dealt with provocative topics, such as climate change or race relations.

There were some tense discussions about the curriculum, but both parents and educators were able to work together in Twin Falls and come to appreciate each other. J.D. Davis, chair of the English department at Twin Falls High School, was initially furious about the state law requiring parental participation, but he says he found the process "not threatening." Chris Reid, a father of seven and a curriculum committee member, was open to hearing other perspectives and was glad to be able to give his. He also admits that "teachers are not evil. They are not trying to indoctrinate my child."

Quoted in Laura Pappano, "Who Picks School Curriculum? Idaho Law Hands More Power to Parents," Hechinger Report, August 14, 2023. https://hechingerreport.org.

protect young people from viewpoints they are not ready to handle. “Having sexualized personal discussions between educators and students in our classrooms are not appropriate, and they can rob our children of their innocence while imposing suggested influence over their developing young minds,”[37] said Louisiana state representative Dodie Horton.

Louisiana is not alone in issuing curriculum restrictions. According to the National Education Association, between April 2021 and January 2023, eighteen states enacted policies regulating the teaching of “divisive concepts” in public schools. On April 28, 2022, for example, Georgia governor Brian Kemp signed House Bill 1084, referred to as the Protect Students First Act, into law. The legislation similarly limits discussions of “divisive concepts.” While the law clearly regulates how racial topics are presented in classrooms, the law’s language is not as explicit when it comes to how sexuality should be handled. Critics say that the imprecise wording puts undue pressure on teachers. “Whenever laws are vague and confusing, and teachers and educators face fear of violating something, it has the result of silencing speech,”[38] says Brock Boone, an attorney with the Southern Poverty Law Center.

A Teacher Is Fired

After the Georgia law went into effect, the state’s teachers were potentially at risk when they discussed anything that touched on sexuality. In March 2023 students in Katie Rinderle’s fifth-grade class asked her to read *My Shadow Is Purple* aloud during their regular reading session. Rinderle had bought the book for her classroom library because she liked the book’s message of being yourself and respecting others who might be different. After some parents objected to the book’s larger theme of tolerance for diverse gender identities, Rinderle was fired on the grounds that she did not follow district policies governing the teaching of “divisive concepts.”

Rinderle’s attorneys argued that the language of the policies was so unclear that no teacher could be expected to know what

Georgia teacher Katie Rinderle (preparing to testify at her 2023 hearing) was fired for reading a book to her fifth-grade class. She said she liked the book's message of being yourself and respecting others, but school officials said the book violated district policy.

was considered acceptable classroom discussion. "For parents to be able, with a political agenda, to come in from outside the classroom and have a teacher fired is completely unfair. It's not right. It's terrible for Georgia's education system,"[39] says Rinderle's lawyer, Craig Goodmark. But supporters of the decision to terminate Rinderle saw it as necessary to keep controversial content away from children in public schools. Sherry Culves, a lawyer for the school district, says, "The Cobb County School District is very serious about the classroom being a neutral place for students to learn. One-sided instruction on political, religious or social beliefs does not belong in our classrooms."[40]

Laws like Protect Students First and Let Kids Be Kids restrict what teachers can discuss when it comes to race, gender, and other topics considered divisive by elected leaders or district administrators. As Rinderle discovered, a teacher who violates the law unintentionally can still be penalized.

"One-sided instruction on political, religious or social beliefs does not belong in our classrooms."[40]

—Sherry Culves, Georgia school district lawyer

Self-Censoring Teachers

According to research released in February 2024 by the Rand Corporation, two-thirds of K–12 public school teachers chose to restrict their lessons on political and social issues—or to self-censor. This self-censorship trend is not limited to states that already have restrictive education policies on the books. Even in states without such prohibitions, 55 percent of teachers still opted to curtail classroom instruction on political and social topics. Some teachers chose to limit their classroom discussions on their own because they feared being harassed by parents and wanted to prevent confrontation, the Rand research found. Others worried that their school or district leaders would not support them if a parent complained, and they did not want to risk losing their job. The consequences of these decisions are widespread. As Rinderle says, "The school board's decision to fire me undermines students' freedom to learn and teachers' ability to teach."[41]

> **"The school board's decision to fire me undermines students' freedom to learn and teachers' ability to teach."[41]**
>
> —Katie Rinderle, Georgia elementary school teacher

Lawmakers, administrators, teachers, and parents have all participated in the battle over what can be discussed during class. But students are also insisting that they deserve to have a say in their education. High school students like Ayesha, a woman of color in California, found it hard to relate to the history she was being taught, and she did not want others to feel similarly left out. She says she thought removing material that would help young people understand their background was "really harmful to students, especially youth who are trying to find their sense of community and where to belong."[42]

Sophia, a New York high schooler, recognizes that history is more complicated than some people make it out to be. She thinks that being exposed to different experiences is essential. "Having access to all viewpoints allows me to expand my knowledge and makes learning a lot more interesting,"[43] she says. Anjali from

Curriculum Adversaries

In August 2023 a group of teachers, parents, and students sued the Temecula Valley Unified School District in California over disputed classroom material. In December 2022 the school board banned the teaching of critical race theory, a college-level topic that deals with racial inequality in American history—even though the theory had never been taught in California K–12 schools. Then in July 2023 the board prohibited social studies textbooks that referenced Harvey Milk, the first openly gay man to be elected to public office in California. Some who objected to the textbooks also thought that they did not adequately celebrate America's unique position in the world. "I don't see all the things we need to see. I don't see a fair and balanced viewpoint. I don't see the civics," says board member Jennifer Wiersma. The board backed down on the textbook issue after Governor Gavin Newsom threatened to fine the county $1.5 million because the board was not following the state-approved curriculum. In the words of California attorney general Rob Bonta, "Restricting what our children are taught in school based on animus or ideological opposition contradicts our societal values."

Quoted in Diana Lambert et al., "Temecula Board Again Votes to Reject Textbooks, Despite Warnings from Newsom," EdSource, July 19, 2023. https://edsource.org.

Pennsylvania believes that those in charge of education should give students more credit for what they can handle. "We need to have the opportunity to explore our knowledge at a deeper level and not be restricted by adults that think that we're not smart enough to understand,"[44] says Anjali.

Well-meaning people can disagree on historical events, gender issues, or any kind of controversial topic. Some believe that children are not prepared to discuss topics that might make them feel uncomfortable, guilty, or forced to accept a viewpoint they do not share. Others maintain that such feelings are part of a young person's quest to find answers, to find their place in society, and to understand the history that has shaped that identity. In her testimony before a congressional committee, school librarian Samantha Hull said, "Any discomfort that arises from what we read is outweighed by the possibility of learning. If the book makes you uncomfortable, it's time to consider what it might be trying to teach you and what you are fighting so hard not to learn."[45]

Regulating Online Speech

In early September 2024 a resident of Springfield, Ohio, named Erika Lee heard a disturbing story from her neighbor Kimberly Newton. According to Lee, Newton had mentioned that a cat belonging to a friend of her daughter had gone missing but was later seen strung up for butchering in a neighboring yard. That yard supposedly belonged to a Haitian immigrant family.

A large influx of Haitian immigrants had settled in Springfield recently to escape the violence and chaos engulfing their island home. They liked Springfield's lower cost of living and the availability of jobs. By most accounts, the Haitians were melding peacefully into the community, and Springfield authorities vouched that most of the immigrants were in the United States legally.

Lee posted the rumor that the Haitians had been involved in the animal's disappearance. After she could find no proof afterward that the cat had been abducted, Lee deleted her post. Newton later said that the cat story was told to her by an acquaintance, not her daughter, and that Lee had misrepresented her comments. But these retractions came too late. The story had taken on a life of its own. It was disseminated across social media at lightning speed, spreading lies that Haitians were stealing and eating neighbors' pets. The unsubstantiated story was given new strength when it was repeated on the campaign trail by the Republican nominee for vice president, J.D. Vance, and was highlighted by Donald Trump during his presidential debate against Democratic opponent Kamala Harris.

Fearing for the safety of his constituents, Rob Rue, the mayor of Springfield, declared repeatedly that there was no truth to these accusations. However, the city faced bomb scares, school closings, and harassment of the Haitian population after Vance and Trump endorsed the unfounded rumor. "It's really unfortunate that our residents have had to endure the impact that they have, especially based off of false claims and false narrative that we have seen here during this presidential election cycle,"[46] said Bryan Heck, the Springfield city manager.

Social media platforms have become a crucial way for people to communicate, get informed, and express themselves. But as the Springfield experience demonstrates, the enormous amount of false and misleading information that circulates so quickly and easily online can unleash panic, endanger the lives of innocent people, and tap into racial prejudice.

A mural in downtown Springfield, Ohio, honors civil rights activist Hattie Moseley. Springfield's Haitian immigrant community was victimized in 2024 by a false story that spread on social media and was in turn repeated during the presidential campaign by J.D. Vance and Donald Trump.

Misinformation and Disinformation

There are distinct types of information that are questionable or that should not be taken at face value. The American Psychological Association, for example, has defined two of these categories. Something that is factually inaccurate is considered misinformation, as in a person who says they were misinformed when they spoke because they got their facts wrong. The second type is disinformation. In this case, people or organizations relay information they know to be false with the purpose of misleading others. For example, when Erika Lee spread the rumor about Haitians stealing cats in Springfield without evidence, she was misinformed, and she took steps to correct the error. But those who continued to spread and then amplify the rumor even after it had been publicly and repeatedly debunked were engaged in a campaign of disinformation for their own purposes.

In the sharing of facts and falsehoods online, the latter has a clear advantage. A study done by the Massachusetts Institute of Technology found that "false news stories are 70 percent more likely to be retweeted than true stories are. It also takes true stories about six times as long to reach 1,500 people as it does for false stories to reach the same number of people."[47] Social media platforms themselves are also part of the reason for the rapid spread of what has come to be referred to as "fake news." Researchers at the University of Southern California noted a simple reason that fake news spreads quickly on social media platforms: the more an individual posts or shares fake news, the more that user is rewarded with increased attention, or "traffic," to his or her social media account—particularly when the claims in the post are outrageous or extreme. Just as a video game has incentives for gamers to keep playing, the researchers found, so too do social media platforms incentivize frequent posts and shares regardless of whether the content is accurate. "Once habits form, information sharing is automatically activated by cues on the platform without users considering critical response outcomes, such as spreading misinformation,"[48] the researchers write.

Weaponizing Social Media

Patrice Motz had been a dedicated Spanish teacher for fourteen years at Great Valley Middle School in Malvern, Pennsylvania. In early 2024 her life was turned upside down when she became a victim of cyberbullying by students. Some eighth graders opened a fake TikTok account in her name and began posting crude content that supposedly came from Motz. One was a real vacation image of Motz at the beach with her husband and children—superimposed with text saying that she liked touching young kids. Motz was one of about twenty teachers at the school who were targeted. The fake images and videos branded the teachers as pedophiles, racists, and homophobes. Some students were suspended, but they claimed that they were only joking and that everyone should get over it. Shawn Whitelock, a social studies teacher who found a fake picture of himself marrying a male student, did not see the humor. "An impersonator assassinated my character—and slandered me and my family in the process," he says. The district superintendent said that there was not much he could do, since students enjoyed wide free speech protection outside of school hours. For Patrice Motz, though, the students' actions made her feel like she had been "kicked in the stomach."

Quoted in Natasha Singer, "Students Target Teachers in Group TikTok Attack, Shaking Their School," *New York Times*, July 6, 2024. www.nytimes.com.

The Limits of Content

Though spreading lies and vile comments might be unethical, regulating fake, derogatory, or hateful speech online is the subject of ongoing debate. Some say that social media platforms should be treated like newspapers and other publications. A newspaper is responsible for ensuring that the content it publishes is accurate and truthful to the best of its abilities. A newspaper that knowingly publishes falsehoods that defame an individual can be sued for libel. Newspaper editors make judgments every day about what content to publish and what to omit. Some insist that content on social media platforms should be policed and even taken down in cases of misinformation or disinformation. The largest platforms have long asserted that they have programs to flag or remove misinformation. However, even this is changing. In January 2025, for instance, Meta CEO Mark Zuckerberg announced that Facebook will no longer use outside fact checkers to police content. Instead, it will rely on users to add notes to posts.

This change appeals to those who believe that users should be able to post any lawful speech they want on their social media accounts. These individuals argue that neither social media companies nor government authorities have the right to edit or remove any content if it falls within the realm of free speech. Anything less would be a form of censorship.

Censorship vs. Public Safety

The debate over whether online speech should be unfettered or regulated took on a new urgency in 2021. On January 6 of that year, after a string of inflammatory tweets, then-president Donald Trump urged his followers to march to the US Capitol to protest the certification of the 2020 election results. Some members of the crowd stormed the building, damaged property, injured police officers, and disrupted a legislative process required by the Constitution. In response to the violence spurred by the tweets, X—as well as Facebook and Instagram—canceled Trump's account. The Capitol assault was widely denounced, but Twitter's action drew criticism and charges of censorship. "We understand the

The debate over regulating online speech took on new urgency in January 2021. Responding to inflammatory tweets by then-president Donald Trump, his supporters stormed the Capitol, damaged property, injured police officers, and disrupted certification of the election.

desire to permanently suspend him now, but it should concern everyone when companies like Facebook and Twitter wield the unchecked power to remove people from platforms that have become indispensable for the speech of billions—especially when political realities make those decisions easier,"[49] said Kate Ruane, a senior legislative counsel at the American Civil Liberties Union.

Some argued that canceling Trump's account was not censorship but an act of public safety to prevent incendiary tweets from leading to more violence. In a different set of circumstances later in 2021, the question of public safety, free speech, and censorship became contentious issues for the Biden administration. As vaccines for COVID-19 were being rolled out, skeptics were posting doubts about their safety on Facebook and other social media sites. The Biden administration argued that spreading misinformation about the coronavirus vaccine would endanger people's lives. Officials like surgeon general Vivek Murthy said that Facebook should be doing more to curtail and even remove misinformation from its site. Meta (formerly Facebook) chief executive officer Mark Zuckerberg claimed that the Biden administration "repeatedly pressured our teams for months to censor certain COVID-19 content, including humor and satire, and expressed a lot of frustration with our teams when we didn't agree."[50]

"[The Biden administration] repeatedly pressured our teams for months to censor certain COVID-19 content, including humor and satire, and expressed a lot of frustration with our teams when we didn't agree."[50]

—Mark Zuckerberg, chief executive officer of Meta

Louisiana and Missouri sued the Biden administration, charging that its efforts to have posts taken down—even though they contained misinformation or disinformation—violated the free speech rights of Facebook users. The government disagreed, arguing that it had the right to discuss content moderation policies with social media companies, especially when erroneous information was being promulgated during a public health emergency. In a 6–3 ruling, the US Supreme Court ruled against the states but left the door open for future litigation.

Censoring Criticism

The National Institutes of Health (NIH) is a government agency that conducts research to improve the health and longevity of Americans. Some of this research involves the use of animals for scientific testing. When animal rights supporters began criticizing the NIH on the agency's social media pages, those comments disappeared. The NIH was using software that automatically blocked keywords that animal activists used to protest the testing. Any post containing words such as *torture*, *testing*, *animal*, *monkey*, and *primate* were deleted from the site, making it seem as if no one objected to the agency's animal testing.

Organizations including People for the Ethical Treatment of Animals sued the NIH for blocking their keywords—and therefore their criticism—on the grounds that it violated First Amendment free speech protections. In July 2024 the US Court of Appeals for the DC Circuit ruled against the NIH. The court said, in part, that government agencies must "tread carefully when enforcing any speech restriction to ensure it is not viewpoint discriminatory and does not inappropriately censor criticism or exposure of government actions."

Quoted in Knight First Amendment Institute, "Federal Court Says National Institutes of Health Censored Critics on Social Media in Violation of First Amendment," July 30, 2024. https://knightcolumbia.org.

Protecting Young People

Over the years, Congress has enacted legislation to regulate online speech and content deemed inappropriate for minors. Some of these laws were struck down by the courts because of their vague wording or because they went too far in limiting First Amendment rights, but others withstood judicial review. In the 2003 case *United States v. American Library Association*, for example, the US Supreme Court held that the government could require any public library that received federal funding to install filtering software on their public computers to block obscene or pornographic images from minors—without being considered censorship.

Passing laws to protect children from the dangers of the internet has been a slow-moving process. The last time Congress agreed on such legislation was in 1998—six years before Facebook and eight years before Twitter were even founded. But in 2022 a new bill was first introduced to deal with the risks young people face on the internet today. Called the Kids Online Safety Act, or KOSA, the proposed legislation would require tech companies to set up safeguards to shield children from online content arguably detrimental to their overall well-being. Anything having to do with bullying, violence, suicide promotion, sexual exploitation, substance abuse, and eating disorders would be among the content affected.

The bipartisan bill, which has been revised and reintroduced since 2022, has been both praised and condemned. Big tech companies such as Microsoft, X, and Snap have thrown their support behind KOSA, applauding the use of reasonable measures to block negative information and images. "We must protect youth safety and privacy online and ensure that technology—including emerging technologies such as AI [artificial intelligence]—serves as a positive force for the next generation,"[51] says Brad Smith, president of Microsoft.

But not everyone agrees that KOSA should become law. Meta's Zuckerberg has yet to support it, saying that the bill's broad restrictions on content are a form of censorship and violate the

"We must protect youth safety and privacy online and ensure that technology—including emerging technologies such as AI [artificial intelligence]—serves as a positive force for the next generation."[51]

—Brad Smith, president of Microsoft

Supporters of the Kids Online Safety Act, which would require tech companies to shield children from harmful online content, deliver a petition to Congress in 2024. The petition, with a hundred thousand signatures, urges passage of the law.

> **“We live on the internet, and we are afraid that important information we’ve accessed all our lives will no longer be available. Regardless of your political perspective, this looks like a censorship bill.”[53]**
>
> —Anjali Verma, high school student

First Amendment. Others are worried that a provision in the bill could hinder kids from accessing sensitive information about things like LGBTQ issues and reproductive rights. In December 2024 nearly thirty organizations sent an open letter to lawmakers such as House minority leader Hakeem Jeffries urging them to oppose KOSA. “The bill’s duty of care provision would give the FTC [Federal Trade Commission] power to bring cases against companies that feature information about sexual orientation and gender identity, arguing that it is harmful to children,”[52] the letter said in part.

Young people, whose lives will be most directly affected by KOSA, are also weighing in on the bill’s passage. In July 2024 more than three hundred high school students mentored by the American Civil Liberties Union journeyed to Capitol Hill. They met with the staff of eighty-five lawmakers to express their opposition to KOSA becoming law, saying it would ban online discussions of issues important to youth. “We live on the internet, and we are afraid that important information we’ve accessed all our lives will no longer be available. Regardless of your political perspective, this looks like a censorship bill,”[53] said Anjali Verma, a seventeen-year-old activist. As of November 2024, KOSA had passed the US Senate with the overwhelming support of Democrats and Republicans but had stalled in the House of Representatives.

The challenge of regulating online speech without slipping into irresponsible censorship is daunting. Tech tools empower practically everyone to create and distribute content to a global audience within seconds. Yet the companies who run these platforms have taken steps to moderate some of that content. Whether those regulations do enough is still the subject of debate. In the end, any form of regulation will mean the suppression of some speech, ensuring that the fight over the limits of free expression will continue.

Free Speech Battles on College Campuses

College campuses have traditionally been places where students from diverse backgrounds come together to gain knowledge, acquire critical-thinking skills, and connect with people with different experiences from their own. Debate and demonstrations over topical issues have always been part of college life. In the 1960s many students protested the Vietnam War, and in the 1980s campuses spoke out against apartheid in South Africa. Recently, universities have seen an increase in student protests—not just over global events but also over the fundamental right to speak and hear various viewpoints. The spike has created tension for campus leaders, who are caught between ensuring free speech rights and providing a safe learning environment for students.

Limits to Free Expression

The conflict between these two ideals is due in part to confusion over what constitutes protected speech. In general, the First Amendment on college campuses covers the speech of faculty and students, even when that speech is arguably repugnant, bigoted, or offensive. But the First Amendment is applied differently at public schools than it is at private schools. Public colleges and universities get their funding primarily from the state. So if school administrators tried to clamp down on expression, it would equate to censorship by the government. This freedom makes it possible for students and faculty to vigorously explore ideas and express themselves without fear that they will be censored. Students at private schools usually do not have the same wide-ranging First

Amendment protections. Private institutions generally respect the First Amendment, but they can also set their own speech policies for their college community. Failure to comply with their guidelines could result in some form of disciplinary action.

Nonetheless, the First Amendment does not offer blanket protection to every kind of speech or behavior under the guise of free expression, whether it occurs on a college campus or elsewhere. Certain categories of speech are not constitutionally protected, and anyone who violates them could be subject to legal action. One such category of unprotected speech involves true threats, which is when someone says that they intend to harm another person or group. For example, in the fall of 2023, police arrested Patrick Dai, a twenty-one-year-old junior at Cornell University. According to the US Attorney for the Northern District of New York, Dai had posted violent threats online against Jewish people, including allegedly threatening "to 'stab' and 'slit the throat' of any Jewish males he sees on campus, to rape and throw off a cliff any Jewish females, and to behead any Jewish babies."[54]

Incitement—that is, when the intent of the speech is to lead to imminent violent or unlawful action—is also not protected by the First Amendment. On May 7, 2024, at the University of Massachusetts, Amherst, students were occupying an encampment on the college grounds during their protests of the Israel-Hamas war, demanding that the university divest itself from any financial ties to Israeli companies. Authorities claimed that the encampment on campus space was illegal and ordered it removed. Police who were called in to oversee that order said that Rüya Hazeyen and Maysoun Batley of Students for Justice in Palestine were inciting the students to riot. According to police, the two were "encouraging people on the periphery of the protest to surround or 'protect' the encampment"[55] from being dismantled. Although the police eventually dropped their allegations in August, the two students could have faced a two-and-a-half year jail sentence if convicted.

Protesters at the University of Massachusetts, Amherst, face off against police in April 2024. A week later, the university removed what it said was an illegal student encampment tied to protests of Israel's response to the October 2023 attack by the Palestinian group Hamas.

Student Safety and the Right to Protest

Every student on campus has the right to pursue their education in a reasonably safe environment and to express themselves in ways that comply with the First Amendment. Any form of bullying, for example, can disrupt a person's educational experience. Therefore, students whose speech or actions contribute to creating a hostile environment may be charged with harassment—an exception to free speech protections under the First Amendment.

The obligation of US colleges and universities to provide safe learning environments and, at the same time, respect free speech rights faced tough challenges after Israel and Hamas went to war in October 2023. In the days and weeks that followed, demonstrations erupted on campuses like the University of Massachusetts, Amherst, between pro-Israeli and pro-Palestinian students—some of whom reported incidents of harassment. For example, on October 31 a Muslim student at the University of North Carolina at Chapel Hill was allegedly attacked at knifepoint by an individual draped in an Israeli flag.

And a twenty-four-year-old Jewish student at the School of General Studies at Columbia University in New York City was posting flyers with the names and photos of Israeli hostages taken by Hamas when he was attacked by someone with a stick. "Freedom of speech is a fundamental value we hold dear, one that fosters intellectual growth, critical thinking, and the exploration of different perspectives. However, it is crucial to emphasize that with this freedom comes the responsibility to ensure that our campus remains safe,"[56] wrote Dennis A. Mitchell, the interim provost, in an email to the entire Columbia University community.

School leaders were compelled to devise strategies to address the conflict between free expression and student safety. At Indiana University, Bloomington, for example, pro-Palestinian protesters intended to build an encampment on a piece of school property traditionally set aside for free expression. But the night before the full encampment went up, school leaders revised their policies, saying that temporary structures were prohibited without approval in advance from the administration—something the protesters claimed they were not notified about. Indiana State Police were sent in to clear the area, arresting more than thirty protesters. School leaders argued that every student was required to follow policy, but others saw it as an attack on free expression. "The fact that they did it late at night, the night before they knew that this pro-Palestine event was scheduled to take place tells us that this was not about security. It was about stifling speech on this particular issue,"[57] said David McDonald, chair of the university's Department of Folklore and Ethnomusicology. Brown University tried a different approach to tone down the conflict on its campus. In exchange for the student protesters ending their encampment, school leaders

"Freedom of speech is a fundamental value we hold dear, one that fosters intellectual growth, critical thinking, and the exploration of different perspectives. However, it is crucial to emphasize that with this freedom comes the responsibility to ensure that our campus remains safe."[56]

—Dennis A. Mitchell, interim provost at Columbia University

Regulating Teachers

In July 2024 Indiana enacted a new law to regulate how and what college professors at public universities could teach. The law requires faculty members to "foster a culture of free inquiry, free expression, and intellectual diversity." The state senator behind the law said the intent was to ensure that professors enlarge the range of viewpoints in their classroom discussions. But instead of promoting free speech, some professors argue that it would stifle their First Amendment rights. They contend that the law is "impermissibly vague" and that the university has offered no guidance on what viewpoints teachers would need to include—making it nearly impossible to know how to comply. Students and employees could lodge complaints against teachers for noncompliance. Even if the complaints are without merit, teachers would still be subject to a time-consuming and onerous investigation. Some worry that faculty will refrain from teaching controversial subjects, rather than face the threat of an investigation. Teachers at Indiana University, Bloomington, and Purdue University have brought a lawsuit against the legislation. "If the state can tell you what you can and can't teach, that cuts to the core of someone's academic freedom," said American Civil Liberties Union attorney Stevie Pactor, who is handling the case.

Quoted in Brian Rosenzweig, "Indiana Passed a Law to Promote Free Speech in Class. A Lawsuit Says It Does the Opposite," *Bloomington (IN) Herald-Times*, October 9, 2024. www.heraldtimesonline.com.

allowed them to meet with the school's governing body to discuss students' demands for withdrawing the university's financial investment in the warring parties' businesses.

The Line Between Abhorrent and Threatening Speech

Sorting out free speech issues is both complex and confusing for students. Max Zimmerman, a student at Towson University studying to become a dentist, believes strongly in the First Amendment. But in the wake of the October 7, 2023, Hamas attack, he felt intimidated as a Jewish student on campus. For example, on the chalkboard at Freedom Square—a public space at Towson devoted to free expression—anti-Israel statements began popping up frequently. Campus protesters had also chanted "from the river to the sea," an expression that is interpreted

> "What I always hear now is how, when students are upset or offended, they phrase it as, 'I feel unsafe.' And I think it's so important that we separate out the campus' duty. It's not our role to make them feel safe from ideas that they don't want to be exposed to. But that line, I think, has gotten blurred."[59]
>
> —Erwin Chemerinsky, dean of University of California, Berkeley, School of Law

by some as a threat to the existence of the Jewish people. "A phrase that has a hidden phrase, like calling for the mass genocide of the Jews, stuff like that shouldn't be allowed on college campuses. There needs to be a limit to what you can say,"[58] Zimmerman said.

Despite the controversy over its meaning, legal scholars such as Erwin Chemerinsky, dean of the law school at the University of California, Berkeley, insist that the phrase is protected speech under the US Constitution. "What I always hear now is how, when students are upset or offended, they phrase it as, 'I feel unsafe.' And I think it's so important that we separate out the campus' duty. It's not our role to make them safe from ideas that they don't want to be exposed to. But that line, I think, has gotten blurred,"[59] Chemerinsky said.

The debate over protecting students' safety and ensuring their First Amendment rights has spread beyond college campuses.

Max Zimmerman, a student at Towson University, said he felt intimidated by statements being chanted during anti-Israel protests on campus.

Cancel Culture Evolves

In August 2024 Professor Samuel J. Abrams of Sarah Lawrence College was discussing the courses he would be teaching in the upcoming fall semester. Students could log in to his Zoom session to hear about the syllabi to help them decide which courses to enroll in. When the session ended, a student alerted Abrams to a private message the student—and presumably all the other Zoom participants—had received. The message distorted Abrams's beliefs, calling him racist and misogynistic. It said that his support of Israel's right to exist and defend itself was equal to supporting the killing of thousands of Palestinian civilians. The message also implied, untruthfully, that he equated supporters of diversity, equity, and inclusion efforts with Nazis. Groups such as Sarah Lawrence's Divestment Coalition were calling for a boycott of his classes. By the next day the number of students enrolled in his courses was significantly lower than usual. "While protesting a professor in the public sphere is one thing, directly targeting and approaching students through multiple channels raises the stakes, significantly increasing the intimidation for those who refuse to fall in line," Abrams says. "Such a culture is the antithesis of a true collegiate education."

Samuel J. Abrams, "The Dangerous Evolution of Cancel Culture," American Enterprise Institute, August 27, 2024. www.aei.org.

Some members of Congress were disturbed by the way college leaders handled—or as some believe, mishandled—these divisive issues. In December 2023 the presidents of Harvard University, the University of Pennsylvania, and the Massachusetts Institute of Technology were called to testify before the House Committee on Education and the Workforce. Committee members were investigating why more was not being done to combat anti-Semitism on campus and to discipline or even expel the students behind it. The presidents denounced the anti-Semitism but explained that even abhorrent language was constitutionally protected speech. After being criticized for their replies, Claudine Gay of Harvard University and Liz Magill of the University of Pennsylvania resigned their presidencies.

The Spread of Cancel Culture

Even before the start of the Israel-Hamas war, rising concerns about the threat to free expression on college campuses were evident. In the past few years, several speakers who had been invited to speak at various schools were disinvited, or canceled, at the last minute.

At some colleges, speakers were being canceled for holding opinions unrelated to their campus talk. In October 2023 Nina Paley was invited by a teacher at Northeastern University, Oakland, to speak to students in an animation course by video chat. Paley, an illustrator and filmmaker, easily agreed to talk about her animation and storytelling techniques and how she became an animator. But about an hour before the session, Paley got an email from the teacher disinviting her because of Paley's long history of opposing transgenderism. In a tersely worded email, the teacher reiterated the school's policy of inclusion and diversity. Even though Paley had no plans to talk about transgender issues, being canceled was nothing new to Paley. "I will never accept another speaking invitation unless they promise not to do this," she says. "Every time I think, 'good, they don't care, it's blown over,' and EVERY TIME this happens."[60]

Sometimes speakers are canceled today for opinions they expressed in the past, even when those opinions might have been more tolerated at the time. For example, radio and TV commentator Michael Smerconish was disinvited from speaking at the 2024 Dickinson College commencement ceremony. The invitation was withdrawn because of remarks Smerconish made in his book *Flying Blind*, published in 2004—twenty years earlier. In it, Smerconish criticized the Transportation Security Administration (TSA) for not being more aggressive in screening young Arab men who might fit a terrorist profile in the months following the September 11, 2001, attacks. After his speaking engagement was canceled, Smerconish admitted that some of his opinions in 2004 may not have been wisely worded but stood by his faultfinding with lax TSA screening policies.

Restricting Academic Freedom

The past few years have also seen professors on various college campuses expressing concerns about constraints being placed on what they teach and how. According to a survey of college

Students listen attentively to a university lecturer. College and university faculty in many states worry that students will be shortchanged as lawmakers increase efforts to regulate what topics can be taught and how those topics are taught.

faculty conducted by Inside Higher Ed/Hanover Research in the weeks before the November 2024 election, "more than 40 percent said their sense of academic freedom in teaching declined over the last year, and more than 20 percent said the same about academic freedom in research."[61]

That loss of academic freedom is being felt in fundamental ways. At Florida International University (FIU) in Miami, for example, in September 2024 university trustees eliminated twenty-two courses from the school's core curriculum. These are classes that students must choose from to fulfill graduation requirements. The action was taken in response to a 2023 state law that restricted the teaching of any course in which the content might suggest that institutions in the United States were built on racist, sexist, or oppressive beliefs. Although the courses in question could still be taken as electives, some faculty members worried that eventually they would be dropped entirely, cheating students and teachers out of the opportunity for vigorous classroom debate on impor-

"When the state begins to regulate what we can teach at the level of the university, then we have to question whether the university can serve its social function, which is to be a place of free inquiry."[62]

—Katie Rainwater, Florida International University professor

tant topics in American history. "When the state begins to regulate what we can teach at the level of the university, then we have to question whether the university can serve its social function, which is to be a place of free inquiry,"[62] says Katie Rainwater, a professor of sociology at FIU.

In the more than two centuries since the First Amendment was ratified, government authorities and regular citizens have debated its meaning and intent. These arguments have defined the scope and limitations of protected expressions. But in recent years, banning books from library shelves, whitewashing curriculum standards, monitoring online speech, and shutting down diverse viewpoints on college campuses have become prominent issues on the national stage. Some argue that these activities amount to censorship, potentially harming individuals' lives and undermining the spirit of the First Amendment. Others maintain that speech carries consequences and that government or private institutions have the right to regulate it when the potential harm is too great. How to respect an individual's precious right of free expression under the law without trampling on that same right for others is a conversation that likely will never be silenced.

Introduction: The Fight Over the First Amendment

1. Quoted in Governor Ron DeSantis, "Governor Ron DeSantis Signs Bill That Requires Curriculum Transparency," March 25, 2022. www.flgov.com.
2. Quoted in Jeffrey S. Solochek, "DeSantis Signs Bill on Book Selection Rules, School Board Limits," *Tampa (FL) Bay Times*, March 25, 2022. www.tampabay.com.
3. Quoted in Brendan Farrington, "DeSantis Signs Bill Targeting Explicit Books in Schools," AP News, March 25, 2022. https://apnews.com.
4. Quoted in Elizabeth A. Harris and Alexandra Alter, "With Rising Book Bans, Librarians Have Come Under Attack," *New York Times*, June 22, 2023. www.nytimes.com.
5. Abby Smith and Robert Corn-Revere, "FIRE to Supreme Court: Only You Can Protect Free Speech Online," Foundation for Individual Rights and Expression, December 6, 2023. www.thefire.org.
6. Quoted in Ayana Archie, "USC Says It Is Canceling Its Valedictorian Speech Because of Safety Concerns," NPR, April 16, 2024. www.npr.org.

Chapter One: An Essential Right

7. Quoted in "Amdt1.71. Historical Background on Free Speech Clause," Constitution Annotated. https://constitution.congress.gov.
8. Quoted in National Archives, "Silence Dogood, No. 8, 9 July 1722." https://founders.archives.gov.
9. Quoted in *Schenck v. United States*, 249 U.S. 47, 52 (1919).
10. Quoted in *Brandenburg v. Ohio*, 395 U.S. 444 (1969).
11. Quoted in Paul Hond, "The Columbia Guide to the Pentagon Papers Case," *Columbia Magazine*, Spring/Summer 2021. https://magazine.columbia.edu.
12. Quoted in *New York Times Co. v. United States*, 403 U.S. 713 (1971).
13. Quoted in Julia Simon, "Climate Scientist Michael Mann Wins Defamation Case Against Conservative Writers," NPR, February 8, 2024. www.npr.org.
14. Quoted in Jim Vertuno, "The Father of a Six-Year-Old Killed at Sandy Hook Says Alex Jones Made His Life a 'Living Hell,'" *PBS NewsHour*, August 2, 2022. www.pbs.org.

Chapter Two: The Movement to Ban Books

15. Quoted in *Little v. Llano County*, No. 23-50224 (5th Cir. 2024).
16. Quoted in Casey Kuhn, "Library Book Ban Attempts Are at an All-Time High. These Librarians Are Fighting Back," *PBS NewsHour*, April 15, 2024. www.pbs.org.

17. Quoted in Bayliss Wagner, "Librarian's Wrongful Termination Lawsuit Against Llano County Can Move Forward, Judge Rules," *Austin (TX) American-Statesman*, August 29, 2024. www.statesman.com.
18. Quoted in American Library Association, "American Library Association Reports Record Number of Unique Book Titles Challenged in 2023," March 14, 2024. www.ala.org.
19. American Library Association, "About Banned & Challenged Books." www.ala.org.
20. Quoted in PEN America, "New Report Finds Unprecedented Surge in School Book Bans," April 16, 2024. https://pen.org.
21. Quoted in Carmen Nesbitt, "Gov. Cox Signs Bill Making It Easier to Ban Books from Utah Schools Statewide," *Salt Lake Tribune* (Salt Lake City, UT), March 19, 2024. www.sltrib.com.
22. Quoted in Chris Arnold, "13 Books Officially Banned from Utah Public Schools," Fox 13 News, August 6, 2024. www.fox13now.com.
23. Quoted in Amy Beth Hanson and Jesse Bedayn, "Utah Bans 13 Books at School, Including Popular 'A Court of Thorns and Roses' Series, Under New Law," AP News, August 8, 2024. https://apnews.com.
24. Moms for Liberty, "Who We Are," 2024. www.momsforliberty.org.
25. Erum Salam, "Book About Book Bans Banned by Florida School Board," *The Guardian* (Manchester, UK), June 11, 2024. www.theguardian.com.
26. Ronald K.L. Collins, "Moms for Liberty: The Anti-Liberty Book Banning Group—First Amendment News 415," Foundation for Individual Rights and Expression, March 13, 2024. www.thefire.org.
27. Quoted in Eesha Pendharkar, "What Happened When Students Led Fights to Reverse Book Bans," *Education Week*, July 18, 2023. www.edweek.org.
28. Quoted in Pendharkar, "What Happened When Students Led Fights to Reverse Book Bans."
29. Quoted in Luke Lippitt, "Students Speak Out Against Book Banning," Students Protecting Education, November 24, 2022. www.studentsproed.org.

Chapter Three: Censorship in the Classroom

30. Melissa Kay Diliberti et al., "7 Takeaways on How Teachers Are Reacting to Restrictions on Discussing Race and Gender," Brookings Institution, May 16, 2024. www.brookings.edu.
31. Quoted in Diane Rado, "DeSantis Signs 'Intellectual Freedom,' Stop WOKE Law; Critics Say It's Racist and Unconstitutional," Florida Phoenix, April 22, 2022. https://floridaphoenix.com.
32. Quoted in Florida Senate, "CS/HB 7—Individual Freedom." www.flsenate.gov.
33. Quoted in Florida Senate, "CS/HB 7—Individual Freedom."
34. Florida Senate, "CS/HB 7—Individual Freedom."
35. Quoted in Glenn C. Altschuler and David Wippman, "Florida's New Black History Standards Are Misleading and Offensive," *The Hill* (Washington, DC), July 30, 2023. https://thehill.com.
36. Ipsos, "Most Parents Want Classrooms to Be Places of Learning, Not Political Battlegrounds," September 21, 2022. www.ipsos.com.

37. Quoted in Piper Hutchinson, "Louisiana Legislature Passes Bill Restricting Discussion of Gender and Sexuality," Louisiana Illuminator, May 23, 2024. https://lailluminator.com.
38. Quoted in Martha Dalton, "Critics of Georgia's New 'Divisive Concepts' Law Say It Could Cause Confusion," WABE, August 9, 2022. www.wabe.org.
39. Quoted in Jeff Amy, "A Georgia School Board Fires a Teacher for Reading a Book to Students About Gender Identity," AP News, August 17, 2023. https://apnews.com.
40. Quoted in Amy, "A Georgia School Board Fires a Teacher for Reading a Book to Students About Gender Identity."
41. Quoted in Tim Walker, "Why Teachers Self-Censor," *NEA Today*, March 1, 2024. www.nea.org.
42. Quoted in Elisabeth Snyder and Allison Swann, "High School Students Explain Why We Can't Let Classroom Censorship Win," American Civil Liberties Union, August 6, 2024. www.aclu.org.
43. Quoted in Snyder and Swann, "High School Students Explain Why We Can't Let Classroom Censorship Win."
44. Quoted in Snyder and Swann, "High School Students Explain Why We Can't Let Classroom Censorship Win."
45. Quoted in Tim Walker, "Educators Fight Back Against Gag Orders, Book Bans and Intimidation," *NEA Today*, July 28, 2022. www.nea.org.

Chapter Four: Regulating Online Speech

46. Quoted in William Brangham and Mary Fecteau, "How Life in Springfield Has Been Disrupted by Lies About Its Haitian Community," *PBS NewsHour*, September 17, 2024. www.pbs.org.
47. Peter Dizikes, "Study: On Twitter, False News Travels Faster than True Stories," *MIT News*, March 8, 2018. https://news.mit.edu.
48. Quoted in Pamela Madrid, "USC Study Reveals the Key Reason Why Fake News Spreads on Social Media," USC Today, January 17, 2023. https://today.usc.edu.
49. Quoted in Natalie Colarossi, "ACLU Counsel Warns of 'Unchecked Power' of Twitter, Facebook After Trump Suspension," *Newsweek*, January 9, 2021. www.newsweek.com.
50. Quoted in House Judiciary Committee, "Mark Zuckerberg just admitted three things," X, August 26, 2024, 6:44 p.m. https://x.com/JudiciaryGOP/status/1828201780544504064/photo/1.
51. Quoted in Christopher Hutton, "Microsoft President Endorses Online Child Safety Bill Night Before Big Tech Hearing," *Washington Examiner*, January 30, 2024. www.washingtonexaminer.com.
52. Quoted in Julia Shapero, "LGBTQ Advocates Ask Leadership to Torpedo Kids Online Safety Act," *The Hill* (Washington, DC), December 10, 2024. https://thehill.com.
53. Quoted in Cecilia Kang, "How the Kids Online Safety Act Was Dragged into a Political War," *New York Times*, July 30, 2024. www.nytimes.com.

Chapter Five: Free Speech Battles on College Campuses

54. United States Attorney's Office, Northern District of New York, "Cornell Student Arrested for Making Online Threats to Jewish Students on Campus," October 31, 2023. www.justice.gov.
55. Dusty Christensen et al., "UMass Seeking Felony Riot Charges Against Palestine Activists," The Shoestring, August 8, 2024. https://theshoestring.org.
56. Quoted in Liam Stack, "Columbia Closes Campus as Israel-Hamas War Protests Erupt," *New York Times*, October 12, 2023. www.nytimes.com.
57. Quoted in Brian Rosenzweig, "Indiana University Changed Its Policy a Day Before a Protest. Then 33 People Were Arrested," *Indianapolis (IN) Star*, April 27, 2024. www.indystar.com.
58. Quoted in Collin Binkley, "As a New Generation Rises, Tension Between Free Speech and Inclusivity on College Campuses Simmers," AP News, January 13, 2024. https://apnews.com.
59. Quoted in Binkley, "As a New Generation Rises, Tension Between Free Speech and Inclusivity on College Campuses Simmers."
60. Quoted in Jennifer Kabbany, "Feminist Artist's Guest Lecture Canceled for Speaking Out Against Transgender Ideology," College Fix, November 15, 2023. www.thecollegefix.com.
61. Ryan Quinn, "Many Faculty Say Academic Freedom Is Deteriorating. They're Self-Censoring," Inside Higher Ed, November 13, 2024. www.insidehighered.com.
62. Quoted in Vimal Patel, "Republicans Target Social Sciences to Curb Ideas They Don't Like," *New York Times*, November 21, 2024. www.nytimes.com.

Organizations and Websites

American Library Association
www.ala.org
This long-standing organization works to enhance and ensure access to information for everyone. Its website has extensive news and data on issues such as banned and challenged books, literacy, and diversity, equity, and inclusion issues.

Electronic Frontier Foundation (EFF)
www.eff.org
The EFF is focused on defending the rights and liberties of individuals online. Its website has resources to help visitors learn more about their digital rights, including free speech, privacy, transparency and innovation, and illegal surveillance.

Foundation for Individual Rights and Expression (FIRE)
www.thefire.org
FIRE is an organization committed to defending and promoting free speech rights and free thought for all Americans. The FIRE website provides a vast resource library, tool kits, reports, and databases and guides on academic freedom, religious liberty, and due process.

Institute for Free Speech (IFS)
www.ifs.org
The IFS is an organization centered on promoting and defending the First Amendment rights of all citizens, particularly political speech rights. Its website has an indexed library of research and academic writing on topics such as the right to protest, content-based discrimination, and internet speech.

Knight First Amendment Institute
https://knightcolumbia.org
The Knight First Amendment Institute protects free expression and freedom of the press through legal action, research, and public education, particularly as these pertain to the digital age. Its website offers blog posts, video content, a podcast, research papers, and articles on First Amendment issues.

PEN America
https://pen.org
PEN America is a long-established organization dedicated to preserving the right to free expression and defending human rights through the power of the word. Its website has up-to-date resources on campus free speech guides, ways to fight books bans, the threat of disinformation, and more.

For Further Research

Books

Amanda Jones, *That Librarian: The Fight Against Book Banning in America*. New York: Bloomsbury, 2024.

James LaRue, *On Censorship: A Public Librarian Examines Cancel Culture in the US*. Wheat Ridge, CO: Fulcrum, 2023.

Greg Lukianoff and Rikki Schlott, *The Canceling of the American Mind: Cancel Culture Undermines Trust and Threatens Us All—but There Is a Solution*. New York: Simon & Schuster, 2023.

Carla Mooney, *Censorship: What Is It and How Does It Impact Society?* San Diego, CA: ReferencePoint, 2024.

Jonathan Turley, *The Indispensable Right: Free Speech in an Age of Rage*. New York: Simon & Schuster, 2024.

Internet Sources

David Acevedo, "Tracking Cancel Culture in Higher Education," National Association of Scholars, November 7, 2024. www.nas.org.

American Library Association, "Top 10 Most Challenged Books of 2024." www.ala.org.

Foundation for Individual Rights and Expression, "Campus Deplatforming Database," 2024. www.thefire.org.

Justin Gamble, "Race Left Out of Rosa Parks Story in Revised Weekly Lesson Text for Florida Schools Highlights Confusion with Florida Law," CNN, March 22, 2023. www.cnn.com.

Mead Gruver, "Librarians Turn to Civil Rights Agency to Oppose Book Bans and Their Firings," AP News, November 8, 2023. https://apnews.com.

David McCabe, "What to Know About the Supreme Court Arguments on Social Media Laws," *New York Times*, February 26, 2024. www.nytimes.com.

PEN America, "How to Fight Books Bans: A Tip Sheet for Students," 2025. https://pen.org.

Isabelle Taft et al., "Campus Protests Led to More than 3,100 Arrests, but Many Charges Have Been Dropped," *New York Times*, July 21, 2024. www.nytimes.com.

Index

Picture Credits

Cover: ANDRANIK HAKOBYAN/Shutterstock

5: Tribune Content Agency LLC/Alamy Stock Photo
9: Maurice Savage/Alamy Stock Photo
13: Photo 12/Alamy Stock Photo
16: james cheadle/Alamy Stock Photo
19: Maury Aaseng
21: fizkes/Shutterstock
22: Everett Collection Inc/Alamy Stock Photo
28: Daniel Hoz/Shutterstock
30: Bridgeman Images
33: Associated Press
37: R Scott James/Alamy Stock Photo
40: Philip Yabut/Alamy Stock Photo
43: Associated Press
47: Associated Press
50: Associated Press
53: stock_photo_world/Shutterstock

About the Author

Robert Lerose has been a writer since 1994. His magazine articles have appeared in *Highlights*, *Boys' Life*, and *Boys' Quest*. He is the author of four nonfiction books for young people. In 2004 he won the Great American Think-Off, a philosophy competition open to people of all ages. He lives on Long Island, New York. Robert Lerose would like to thank all the remarkable teachers and librarians in his life who helped him become an avid reader, an award-winning writer, and a critical thinker.